MOYRA McNEILL'S
Machine
Embroidery
MADE EASY

MOYRA McNEILL'S
Machine Embroidery
MADE EASY

LITTLE HILLS PRESS CRAFT SERIES

Acknowledgements

In order to write a book like this it is useful to be able to work on more than one brand of sewing machine. My own is a basic Bernina and therefore I would like to express my thanks to Pfaff for loaning me their creative 1473 CD machine which is a marvel of modern technology. Thanks are similarly due to Elna who also lent me a machine.

Author's Note

Measurements in this book are given as rounded equivalents of metric and imperial, however when buying material in metric measurement, you may find a store will only sell fabric to the nearest 10cm.

Follow only the metric or the imperial instructions to avoid confusion in the measurements.

Copyright (c) Moyra McNeill, 1991
Little Hills Press Pty Ltd
Regent House,
37–43 Alexander Street,
Crows Nest, NSW 2065

Tavistock House
34 Bromham Road
Bedford MK40 2QD
United Kingdom

ISBN 1 86315 022 6

Designed by Emma Seymour
Edited by Alice Scott
Colour photography by Suzanne Grundy, Imagetrend Ltd

National Library of Australia
Cataloguing-in-Publication data

McNeill, Moyra.
    Machine embroidery made easy.

    Includes index.
    ISBN 1 86315 022 6.

    1. Embroidery, Machine. I. Title.

746.44028

Printed in Hong Kong

CONTENTS

INTRODUCTION

This book is planned for the person who wants to experiment with machine embroidery and has no access to classes. Many books on machine embroidery describe the 'free' method. This allows great freedom of movement but does mean basic alterations to the machine, which, while simple to the adventurous, can be a trifle daunting to someone who can never see the technique demonstrated. So, in general the techniques in this book require no alteration to the machine but nevertheless develop its potential for decoration.

It is assumed that the reader has an electric sewing machine with straight stitch and zigzag. However, several techniques can be worked with a hand operated machine. In contrast, other methods develop the potential of pattern making which many modern machines offer.

Throughout the book there are instructions for applying the techniques to actual items, so that as well as learning how to do the embroidery, something useful can be made at the same time. For each article specific materials and threads are mentioned as a guide, as well as colour suggestions; but, of course, both materials and colours may be altered depending on both the worker's taste and what is readily available.

This is just the beginning and it is hoped that this book will encourage the reader to go on to other kinds of machine embroidery. Where appropriate, suggestions are made for further experimentation with the technique. For ease of understanding, each procedure is described individually but many can be mixed; for example, appliqué and quilting and tufting could all be mixed on one piece of embroidery. Designs are also offered ready planned, but a great deal of interest and gratification can be added to embroidery when you design your own work. Treat this as a beginning and be prepared to try designing for yourself at a later stage.

Perhaps it should be mentioned that machine embroidery is not a poor relation of hand embroidery; quite to the contrary, it is a craft in its own right. While some processes are similar to the hand embroidered version, there are several which are essentially for the machine. There are notable designer embroiderers who work only in machine embroidery and whose embroidery is of the highest aesthetic quality.

THE MACHINE

Choosing a machine

What machine to buy? Like buying a car it depends on a variety of factors. What do you want it to do? How much money is available? The best thing to do is to list what you want the machine to do; then approach a supplier and find out which machines suit your specifications. Then actually sit down and try the machine; this will sort out which are 'comfortable' and which are not. After all everyone expects a test drive in a car. Also try a variety of materials from very thin to thick, to see if the stitch quality is maintained. Check what the guarantee covers. When you have all your answers you are ready to make a choice.

Try not to be beguiled by all sorts of modern wizardry; aim for quality and reliability wherever possible.

Maintenance

Be prepared to look after your machine with loving care.

Many people have the idea that a machine has a mind and moods of its own, but most faults can be laid at the feet of the operator! One of the most important requirements of a machine is that it needs to be cared for; this means following the instructions of the machine manual to the letter.

When using a machine continuously, the race, which is the mechanism around the bobbin, dries out and needs oiling. It requires only a minimum of oil, literally, just one drop, but applied on a regular basis. If oiling is neglected it can prevent the thread running freely, which makes it break or knot.

Many small fibres are shed by both the thread and fabric while machining and can very quickly hinder the smooth running of the machine; they build up underneath the teeth or feed as thick fluff. Brush this fluff out frequently and the machine will stitch better and last longer.

Do read the machine manual, as most of the manuals list reasons for any malfunction of the machine, whether it be thread breaking or missed stitches. Most importantly, they suggest how to remedy the fault.

Needles

Depending on the material used, needles can blunt quite quickly, and should be changed at frequent intervals. It is not always realised that there are needles for different purposes, as well as a variety of sizes.

Needle sizes vary from 70 [9] to 110 [18], fine to thick. The 110 size is often sold as a 'jeans' needle.

The following are types of needles available:
General sewing needle, i.e. an ordinary needle.
Ballpoint needle for knitted fabrics. It slides between the fibres of a fabric rather than piercing them.

Leather needle; it has a three-sided point to pierce leather easily.

Twin needle; this is just what its name suggests, two needles in a single shaft. It is used for tucking or Italian quilting or cording.

Threads

Domestic sewing machines are designed to work with ordinary sewing threads, which are nowadays manufactured in a variety of fibres; polyester, cotton and pure silk for example. These threads may be used for both practical and decorative work. Bigger reels of 1000 metres are better value than many small reels.

Nowadays, in addition to sewing threads, there are many exciting new threads on the market made specifically for embroidery. Some are made of rayon so that they have a rich, glossy effect, others are lurex with a metallic finish, and there are mixes of rayon and metallic which give a subtle twinkle. A reel of thread may be multicoloured, giving blocks of yellow, green, blue and pink in succession, for example; or it may be graded from light to dark and back again in one colour only. There are also gentle gradations of tone, from dark blue, to emerald, to purple. This means that new horizons have been opened up for machine embroidery, both as regards texture and colour.

In each project, specific threads are suggested but it is hoped that the reader will feel able to also experiment with threads.

Materials

The projects illustrated in this book use a variety of fabrics, from lightweight dress fabrics to heavier furnishing materials. In general the best tempered fabric to work on is a medium weight cotton, such as a sturdy calico. Any material with a very open weave, or lightweight and 'slippery' is more problematical, and not the best one to make a start on.

Interlinings and other ancillary fabrics

Today there are many aids to sewing and embroidery, by way of interlinings which are sold in many weights, and in a range of substances. There are backings that will bond one fabric to another; fabrics that can be used as a temporary stiffening and then torn away; battings [paddings] of differing thicknesses and weights. Unfortunately, their trade names vary from country to country, and therefore a general description is given in the text beside a trade name.

TRANSFERRING DESIGNS

There are many modern aids to transferring designs, which include:

Water dissolvable felt tip pen.

This is usually a bright turquoise blue and disappears when dabbed with a dampened tissue. On some fabrics it does re-emerge when dry so that it needs to be re-dabbed, or in exceptional cases, rinsed. Use as lightly and sparingly as possible in the first place.

Light disappearing pen.

This is often pink in colour and fades with light. Be prepared for it to fade very swiftly in some circumstances.

Dressmaker's pencil.

This is a pencil made of dressmaker's chalk and can be obtained in different colours; blue, white and yellow for example. It is useful for a temporary marking of fabric, and can be brushed off.

There have been some doubts expressed concerning the long term effect of dissolvable pens on fabric, but so far there is no positive proof, to the knowledge of the author, that they damage or rot the fabric. Any new product can only be proven or disproven by time.

Methods of transferring designs

Tracing (diagram 1)

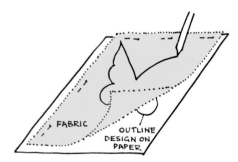

Diagram 1 Transferring a design using the tracing method

1 Draw the outline of the design with a black felt tip pen on white paper.
2 Place the fabric on top of this and pin in position.
3 Trace the design through with any of the pens or the pencil described.
4 Remove the pins and tracing paper.

Many more fabrics than seem likely are transparent enough to use this technique, but the maximum contrast of black pen on white paper is essential for the design to be seen clearly.

Template (diagram 2)

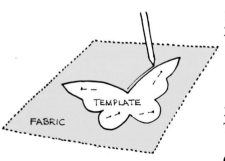

Diagram 2 Transferring a design using a template

1 Draw the design in simple outline twice.
2 Cut one design along the design lines, that is, cut it in pieces. These pieces will form templates which are placed and pinned on the fabric, using the other design to refer to for correct positioning. The templates can then be drawn round or the outline worked in running/tacking stitches.
3 Remove the pins and templates.

This technique is suitable for dark coloured or opaque fabrics.

Chalk method (diagram 3)

1 Draw the outline of the design on paper.

2 Turn the paper over and chalk all over the back. Use the chalk on its side for swifter coverage, or use dressmaker's chalk.

3 Place the fabric on a flat, firm surface, put the design on top, pin in position.

4 With a hard, sharp pencil, follow the outline of the design. Remove the pins and design after making sure all the design lines have been covered. The chalk outline will not last long, but long enough to work most machine techniques.

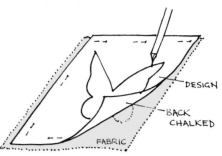

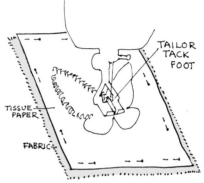

Diagram 3 The chalk method for transferring designs

Tissue paper and tacking method (diagram 4)

1 Trace the outline of the design onto tissue paper.

2 Put tissue paper on top of the fabric and pin in position.

3 Sew small tacking stitches or a running stitch through the paper and fabric, or use the tailor tack foot on the machine if the design is not too intricate.

4 Tear off the paper, leaving the outline of the design in tacking.

This method is suitable for fabrics with a 'hairy' surface. Do not be tempted to use tracing or drawing paper in place of tissue paper, as they will drag the stitching when tearing off.

Warning Never use ordinary pencil, biro or carbon paper as they will all leave permanent marks on the fabric.

Diagram 4 Using tissue paper and tacking to transfer the design

GENERAL TIPS

Stitch tension

People worry too much about ideal stitch tension. As long as the thread lies firmly on both sides of the fabric, without loops or puckering, do not worry. Sometimes it is necessary to alter tension but only by a minimal movement of the tension control at a time. Make sure you understand exactly what you are doing by following the instruction manual for your machine. Some machine embroidery threads, particularly the metallic ones, need the top tension to be slackened, but do it bit by bit.

Testing to save undoing

Machine embroidery can be undone, albeit painstakingly. To save having to undo, make tests on an oddment of fabric exactly the same as that to be used; ensure that the colour, length and width of the stitch are satisfactory before starting on the proper piece. This will save both time and heartache!

Spools

Machine embroidery often uses a lot of thread so make sure the spool is full before starting. Fill two or three spools in preparation if a big piece is to be worked.

Spaced lines

When working lines of stitchery in parallel, whether straight stitch, zigzag or pattern, it is helpful to have some form of guide. Markings on the foot are often provided for this purpose, or markings can be made with a sliver of sticky tape or a felt tip marker.

If a wider spacing is required, cut a piece of card to the right size and use this as a marker in preference to a ruler (diagram 1).

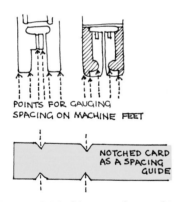

POINTS FOR GAUGING
SPACING ON MACHINE FEET

NOTCHED CARD
AS A SPACING
GUIDE

Diagram 1 Markings on the machine foot provide a spacing guide or a notched card can be used to keep wide stitch lines parallel

Finishing off ends

On most pieces of work it is advisable to finish off the ends neatly and this may be done in the following ways:
1 Tying off. With work on the wrong side, pull the top thread through and tie the bobbin and top thread in a firm knot. Tedious but secure.
2 When starting machining, take two or three stitches forward, then the same backwards, then continue forward. Cut the ends off close to the fabric. Finishing can be done in the same way.
3 When starting or finishing, leave the ends about 3in (7.5cm) long. Thread these in a needle and darn back into the

material, or hide in a seam. Although painstaking, the ends can be quite invisible using this method.

Pressing

Always press embroidery from the wrong side on a soft surface; several layers of blanket, for example.

Never press English quilting, or it will be no longer quilted!

Making up

In this book most of the articles need to be made up. It is not advisable to cut out before the embroidery is complete. Many kinds of embroidery 'shrink' the fabric, so place the pattern pieces on after the decoration is finished, and re-mark seam lines where necessary, before cutting out. Making up is as important as the embroidery, so be prepared to spend as much time on the construction as on the decoration. Accurate and careful making up leads to a professional finish and enhances the total effect.

Enlarging designs

Nearly all the items in this book are provided with a pattern, but you may wish to enlarge or reduce it. The patterns are on squared paper so this may be done by using bigger or smaller squares to draw them up. If you have access to a photocopier which enlarges or reduces, it can do the work in a trice, leaving more time for embroidery!

DEVELOPING STITCH AND PATTERN

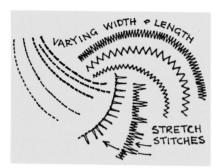

Diagram 1 A variety of stitches can be produced on a basic machine

It is often not realised what a variety of stitches can be produced from a very basic machine. There is a misconception that it is the machine that does the variations and the operator has no further options. This is simply not true. Consider a straight stitch; by making it long it has a different effect than by making it very short, and there are all the differing lengths in between. By machining with a thicker thread [size 40] the stitch is more definite than if a thin thread [size 50 or Madeira Toledo] is used. These are not just minimal differences but show quite clearly (diagram 1).

Basic patterns

Most modern machines are provided with zigzag; as well as varying the stitch length, and the weight of thread, the width can also be altered. With these three permutations a whole range of choices emerge. Although the machine may not have 'patterns', many do have stretch stitches which can be used as patterns. Do not forget that the length, thread, and width can be altered with these as well.

Patterns

Many recent domestic machines have a pattern ability to a greater or lesser extent. If you have such a machine, it is a good idea to make a sampler of the patterns, to decide which you like best.

Wide patterns tend to cockle the cloth, especially if it is thin, and it is a good precaution to support the fabric with a backing that can be removed. This backing can be tissue paper, which is easy to tear away, or stitch 'n tear, which is a cross between paper and felt in appearance, makes a firmer backing and will also tear away. Firm paper such as typing or notepaper is not really suitable as it tends to be too strong and pulls the stitching as it is removed.

If it will make no difference to the work if the backing remains, then iron-on interfacings can be considered, or any interfacing that is strong enough to support the fabric.

Remember that the variations already mentioned of length, width and thread thickness can usually be applied to patterns.

SERVIETTE using basic stitches

Materials

½yd [46cm] of plain cotton [brown] which will make two serviettes.
White sewing cotton 40 or Madeira Tanne [white].

Directions

1 Cut the fabric in half to make two squares.
2 Machine edge first, ½in [1.2cm] from the edge. The scallop is a set pattern on several machines including Bernina and Pfaff, but a plain zigzag would be quite suitable.
3 Mark a line ½in [1.2cm] in from this for the next row of stitching, the stretch stitch.
4 Sew a straight stitch ¼in [6mm] next; then a wide close zigzag another ¼in [6mm] away.
5 Machine a wiggly line, which can be a pattern or a straight stitch, moving the fabric to make it curve close to the zigzag (diagram 1).
6 Trim the edge close to the edge stitching.

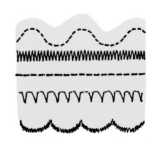

Diagram 1 The pattern of stitches which edge the serviette

TIE using straight stitch, zigzag and stretch stitch

Materials

½yd [46cm] of fabric [fine black wool]. ½yd [46cm] of white
  satin ribbon in three widths 1in, ⅝in, ¼in [2.5cm, 1.5cm,
  6mm].
Black and white sewing thread.
Silver thread [Madeira Astro or similar].
½yd [46cm] tie lining or medium weight cotton fabric.

Directions

1 Mark the outline of the tie on the fabric with tailor's chalk.
2 Tack on the ribbons at the spacing shown, and stitch them
   down with white straight stitch on either edge. Make sure the
   ribbon extends on to the turning so that the ends are hidden
   in making up.
3 Next work the silver stretch stitch lines, the silver satin
   zigzag, and the straight stitch lines. The straight stitch lines
   are worked one row on top of the other to make them bold.
4 Machine the black straight stitch [double] and the stretch
   stitch.
5 Work the white zigzag and straight stitch.

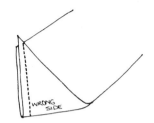

*Diagram 1 Turn in the ends of the
tie, right sides together, and seam*

Making up

1 Press the embroidery from the wrong side on to a soft surface. Cut out the two halves of the tie.
2 Join the centre seam and press flat.
3 Turn in the ends, right sides together, and seam. Trim the
   corners before turning through to the right side. Press (diagram 1).
4 Fold the tie in half lengthwise, right sides together and seam
   (diagram 2).
5 Cut the lining slightly narrower than the finished tie, on the
   cross. Seam two halves.
6 Match the centre of the lining with the seam line of the tie
   and stitch down this line. At this stage it seems unbelievable
   that it will work, but it does (diagram 3).
7 Trim off any superfluous lining, at the ends. Turn the tie
   through to the right side.
8 Press the tie, but before doing so, place a tie shape inside or
   the seam will mark the front of the tie. The tie shape is the
   same as the lining and can be made from cardboard, such as
   a cornflake packet. Press the tie from the back first, and only
   on the front if it seems absolutely necessary.

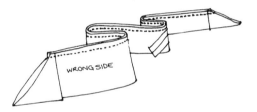

*Diagram 2 Fold the tie in half
lengthways, right sides together, and
seam*

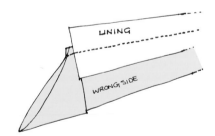

*Diagram 3 Match the centre of the
lining with the seam line of the tie
and stitch down this line*

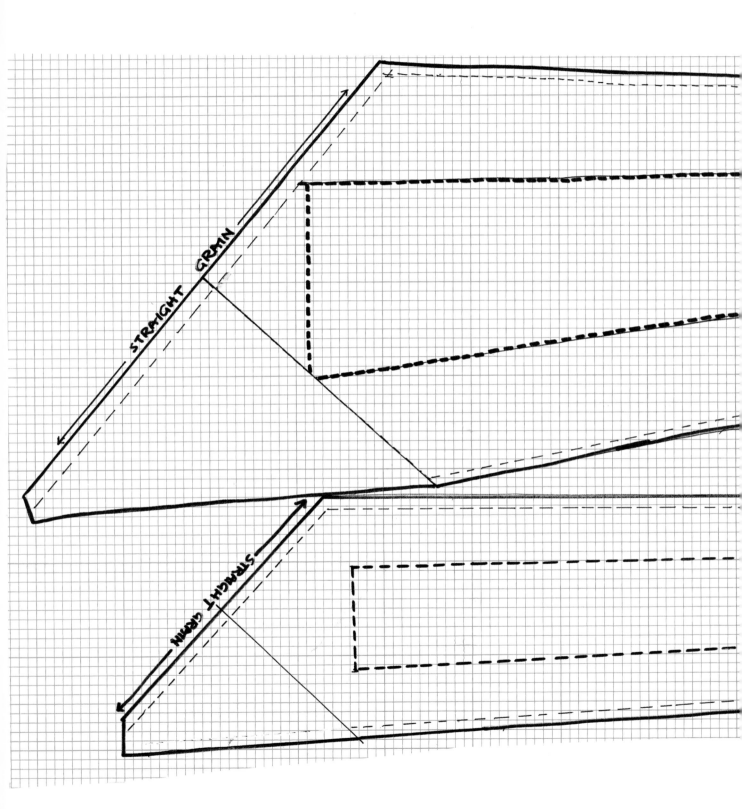

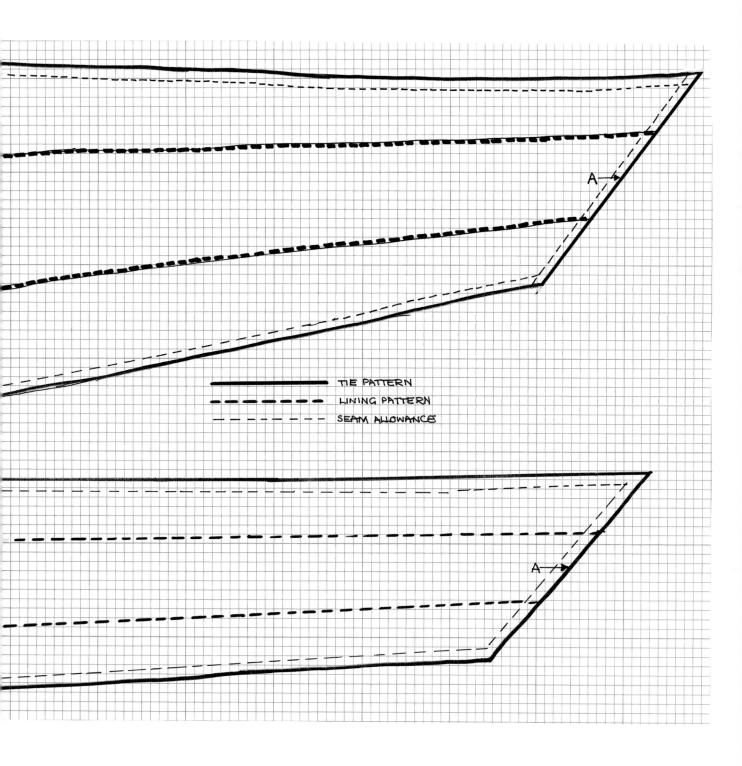

TIE PATTERN

LINING PATTERN

SEAM ALLOWANCE

GLASSES CASE decorated with patterns

The patterns on this item were made on a Pfaff machine, but the idea of almost covering a fabric with patterning could be done with any range of patterns and even very basic ones. So often a single row of pattern is seen in isolation and looks 'thin' but by grouping them together a much richer effect is achieved. When planning this case the aim was to use several dense patterns close together, contrasted with more open spaced patterns.

Materials

A piece of fabric 6in × 15in [15cm × 38cm] such as black silk habotai. Stiff interlining 3 ½in × 13in [9cm × 33cm]; the thickest vilene, pelmet vilene.
Plain gold and multicolour metallic thread [Madeira Astro].
Black sewing thread.
A piece of chamois leather or felt 3in × 12in [7.5cm × 30cm].

Directions

1 Pin the fabric to the backing, matching centre lines. Machine in black down the centre line in straight stitch, to hold the two together.
2 The patterns now worked will depend on your machine. Start from the centre with the richest pattern and work outwards. Fill a strip about 2in [5cm] wide, and alternate the gold and multicolour thread. Working outwards from the centre again, in the other direction, first leave a space of about ½in [1.2cm] and then work two rows of pattern. The spectacle case illustrated used six patterns in all, plus a row of zigzag. The patterns were not worked the full length of the spectacle case, but were stopped ½in [1.2cm] short of the ends.

Making up

1 Turn on to the wrong side, fold the edges of the fabric on to the interlining and stitch in place by hand. Fold the corners neatly (diagram 1).
2 Place chamois or felt centrally and hem in position; it should lie a little bit in from all the edges (diagram 2).
3 Fold in half lengthwise, tack and then machine the side edges together in black straight stitch, ⅛in [3mm] in from the edge. Fasten off very securely (diagram 3).

This idea of grouping patterns together could work well on a belt or pocket top or reveres. It could similarly form the decoration on a bag, or become a textile bracelet.

By experimenting with colour on colour, for example turquoise and blue on purple, a rich and colourful surface texture can be developed.

Need the patterns be side by side? Why not work one on top of the other and see what happens?

Diagram 1 With the right sides of the fabric together, fold the edges on to the interlining and stitch

Diagram 2 The piece of chamois or felt should be placed in the middle of the fabric

Diagram 3 Fold in half lengthwise and sew the side edges together

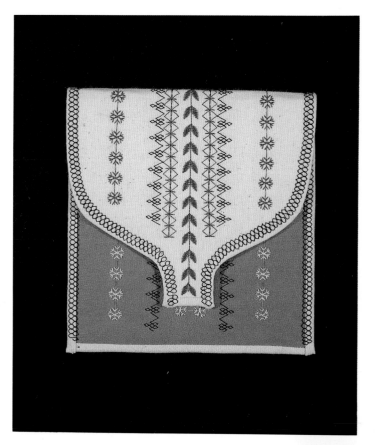

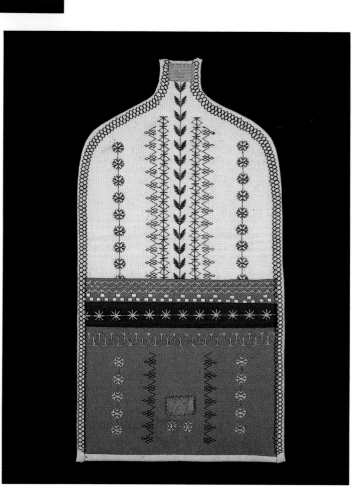

SMALL BAG WITH THREE POCKETS

This small bag uses pattern in a formal way in a symmetrical design. In addition, it uses both sides of the pattern so that the outside and inside are embroidered at the same time. Therefore the stitch tension needs to be well balanced for the pattern to look crisp on both sides.

The idea for the shape of the bag came from an Indian example, and is planned so that several small objects can be contained in a very small area. The pattern could be enlarged to hold much bigger objects.

The bag illustrated is made in plain cottons, but it could be made in silks for a more special look. It could also be lengthened to create a wall hanging with many pockets.

Materials

¼yd [23cm] cream cotton or medium weight calico.
22in × 9in [56cm × 23cm] tan colour cotton.
12in × 9in [30cm × 23cm] dark brown cotton.
Black sewing cotton.
Tan sewing cotton.
Cream sewing cotton.
¼yd [23cm] heavy non-fray interlining [pelmet vilene].
Cream bias binding.
1in [2.5cm] velcro or similar.

Directions

1 Cut the bag shape out of the interlining. Cut a piece of cream fabric twice its length and fold it to cover the interlining (diagram 1). Pin in place and work a pattern right down the centre to hold them together. The patterns on the bag were worked on a Pfaff machine, but choose any appropriate pattern that is available. Then work two patterns either side of the first one; leave a space and work another; repeat on the other side to make it symmetrical.

2 Cut the smallest pocket out of non-fray interlining and cover it with the tan fabric. Work a line of pattern along the folded edge. Then work four lines of pattern at right angles, leaving a space in the middle to sew the velcro to.

3 Cut the material for the remaining two pockets. Slip a 1in [2.5cm] strip of interlining inside the fold, and hold in place with a line of pattern. By not having these pockets fully interlined the bulk is reduced considerably.

Making up

1 Place the main bag shape on a flat surface. On top of it place the three pockets. Pin and tack firmly in position, and straight stitch ⅛in [3mm] from the edge to hold all the pieces together. Trim the edges so that they are level (diagram 2).

2 Bind the edge with bias binding, or a bias strip of cream cotton, enclosing all the raw edges. Work a pattern over the bias strip.

3 Sew on a small piece of velcro to the pocket and flap as a fastening.

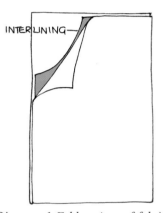

Diagram 1 Fold a piece of fabric over the interlining

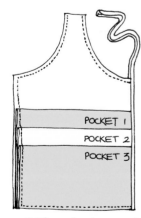

Diagram 2 Place the three pockets on the main bag shape and straight stitch to hold the pieces together

23

*Pattern 2 Small bag with three
pockets*

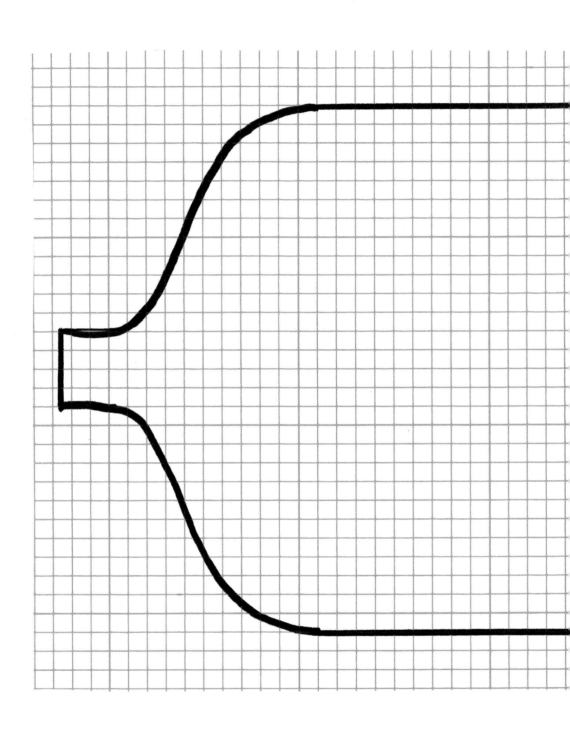

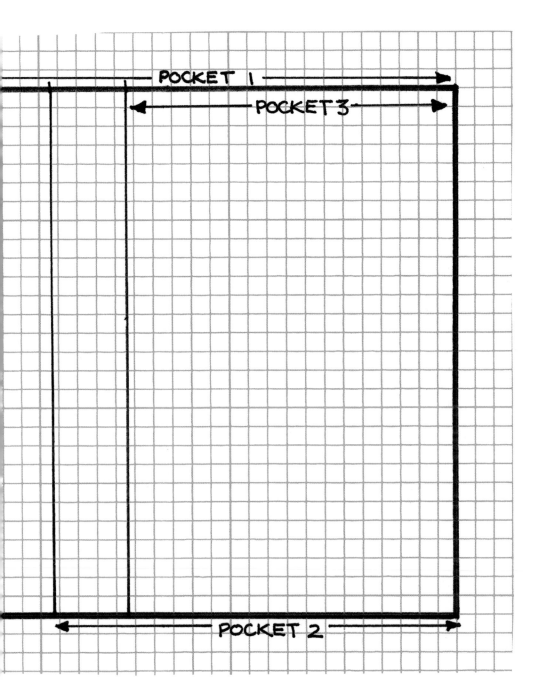

As this pattern is to be cut from thick Vilene
no turnings have been allowed.

KANGAROO BRACES

Many machines nowadays offer patterns based on animals and birds, and the idea of these braces was to utilise such patterns. The design can therefore be based on any animal or bird pattern your machine produces. Instead of kangaroo braces they could equally well be dog, duck or elephant braces! Surely most children, and perhaps teenagers, would be delighted to have braces depicting their favourite animal. To emphasise the message, the name of the animal is written so that it repeats as a pattern. Many machines include a lettering option, which is how the braces illustrated were worked, but letters can equally well be machined free-hand.

The length of materials will depend on the size of the wearer. Measure from the front waistline to the back waistline over the shoulder. Four times this measurement is the length of petersham needed.

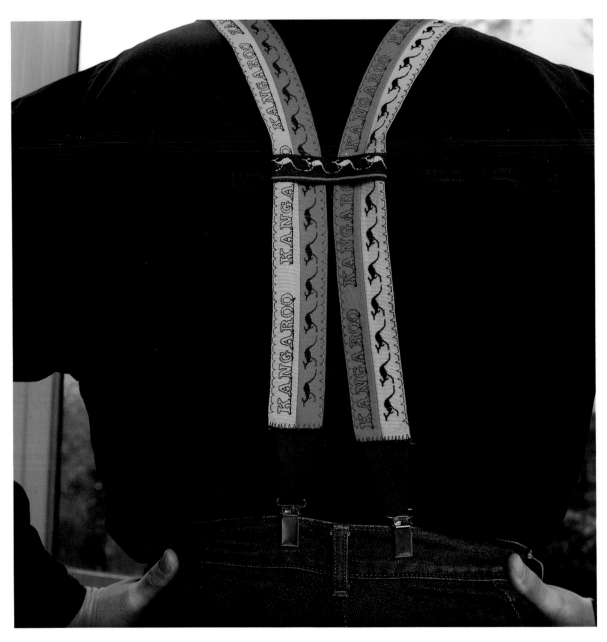

Materials

These materials are for a person approximately 5ft 4in [162cm] tall.

2yd [1.8m] of cerise petersham, or strong ribbon, 1½in [4cm] wide.

2yd [1.8m] of orange petersham, or strong ribbon, 1½in [4cm] wide.

Bondaweb.

1yd [91cm] ½in [1.2cm] wide black elastic.

Black sewing thread.

4 clip on ends for braces.

7½in [19cm] black petersham.

Petersham is a firm ribbed ribbon, but any really firmly woven ribbon or braid could be used as an alternative.

Directions

1 Cut petersham in half, that is four 1yd [91cm] lengths. Put the orange and cerise back to back and sew down the centre. Press the seam open. Turn in the ends.

2 Inside this 'seam' place a ½in [1.2cm] strip of bondaweb. Iron in place. There will be now two lengths of ribbon, half cerise and half orange.

3 Machine the animal of your choice using one colour of petersham, either cerise or orange. Now using the other colour, machine the name of the animal. At this stage the ribbons are likely to twist and cockle. Do not worry.

4 Work a stretch stitch down the outer edges (diagram 1).

5 Cut the elastic into eight equal lengths. Put two lengths through one of the brace ends, tuck the raw ends between the ribbon ends. Tack in place and zigzag right across the ribbon ends, and back again. Machine a stretch stitch above the zigzag. Repeat for the other three ends (diagram 2).

6 Press firmly with a damp cloth, from the wrong side.

7 Make a bar to contain the two straps. Seam the black petersham to form a ring. Fold in half and work a pattern on it.

8 Fold the ring in half and straight stitch down the centre. Place a strap through each half of the ring (diagram 3).

To make sure the lettering will fit, work a sample word on an odd piece of petersham, measure the length of it, and mark how many times it will repeat, adjusting the spaces in between the words accordingly.

Diagram 1 Work a stretch stitch down the outer edges of the braces

Diagram 2 Join elastic to the ribbon through brace ends and stitch together

Diagram 3 Place a strap through each half of the patterned ring

APPLIQUÉ

Appliqué is a very familiar technique to most people, and is particularly suited to machining. If a practical article which is easily laundered is to be made, it is wise to follow common sense rules.

The applied piece of fabric should not be heavier in weight than the background, or pulling can occur.

The applied piece should be the same fibre as the background. For example, if a woollen fabric was applied to a synthetic, it might well cockle when washed.

The grain of the fabric should match that of the background. Nowadays this is not important when an iron-on backing, or bonding agent, is used. There are two alternatives for bonding fabric. One is an interlining which has 'glue' on one side. It is ironed on to the back of the applied pieces and will prevent them fraying. One trade name is Iron-on Vilene which can be obtained in different weights. The other is a bonding agent that is paper backed. This is first ironed on to the applied fabric, the required shapes are cut out and the paper removed. The shapes are then ironed on to the background. Make sure they are in exactly the right place before ironing as the bond is instant. One trade name for this material is Bondaweb. Despite being bonded to the background, it is sensible to stitch the appliqué firmly round the edge for an item that is to be worn and washed (diagram 1).

If a really crisp edge is required, satin stitch is the obvious answer. To prevent it stretching on curves, support it underneath with tissue paper. When a material is bonded to the background, an open zigzag is sufficient to hold it in place. This is useful when the design requires less definite edges to shapes.

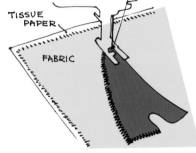

Diagram 1 Stitch the appliqué firmly round the edges and to prevent any stretching on curves, support the material with tissue paper

TABLE MAT WITH CONVOLVULUS DESIGN

Materials

½yd [46cm] cotton fabric, 40in [1m] wide; mid-green.
Small pieces in white and dark green of the same or similar fabric.
White and dark green sewing thread.
Bondaweb.

Directions

1 Cut the mid-green fabric in half to make two 'squares'. Mark the outline of the design on the fabric about 4in [10cm] in from the shorter edge.
2 Iron bondaweb onto the back of the white and dark green fabric.
3 Cut the three leaves and the flower calyx from the dark green fabric. Cut the two flowers from the white material.
4 Remove backing and iron leaves and flowers in position.

28

Pattern 3 Table mat with convolvulus
design

Diagram 1 With right sides together seam around three sides of the mat, turn through to the right side, slip stitch the opening and machine two rows of straight stitch near the edge

5 Sew leaves down with dark green open zigzag.
6 Sew flowers down with white open zigzag.
7 Machine the stem in white zigzag and the veins and tendrils in straight stitch. Machine details on flowers in dark green straight stitch.

Making up

1 Place two squares of material, right sides together. Mark the size of the mat, 18in × 12in [46cm × 30cm] making sure the appliquè is well positioned.
2 Machine round three sides of the marked stitching line, trim the corners and turn through to the right side. Turn in the open side and slip stitch.
3 Machine two rows of straight stitch round the mat, 1/4in [6mm] from the edge (diagram 1).

LARGE BAG IN BRODERIE PERSE

Broderie Perse is a kind of appliqué where the applied pieces are complete motifs from a printed fabric. In other words, sections are cut from a printed fabric such as a flower, or a leaf, or a bird, and then re-arranged on a plain background and stitched in position. Pieces from several different fabrics can be combined on one embroidery, although it would be advisable to choose fabrics which have a colour link, for example, each piece has a particular red in it. In the bag illustrated, the pieces were all cut from a remnant of furnishing fabric and then re-arranged to fit the shape of the bag. When planning like this, where much of the base is hidden, arrange the appliqué where it will show to best effect, that is, on the sides. The technique for applying the motifs is exactly the same as for any appliqué, but remember that the applied pieces should be about the same weight as the background for a practical item.

Materials

¾yd [68cm] of medium weight fabric [furnishing fabric] in a
    plain colour, 54in [137cm] wide.
Sewing thread to match.
About ½yd [46cm] of patterned fabric.
Sewing thread to tone with the above.
¾yd [68cm] lining.
Bondaweb or similar.
2yd [1.8m] petersham or similar, 1 in [2.5cm] wide.

Directions

1 Mark out the shape of the bag in tailor tacking as described in the manufacturer's instruction booklet; that is, two pieces, back and front. Do not cut out yet.
2 Iron bondaweb on the back of the patterned fabric. Cut out the motifs.
3 Arrange the motifs within the bag shape, bearing in mind that the base will not be seen. Remove the backing and iron on the shapes; then zigzag around the edges with a slightly open zigzag.

Making up

1 Cut out bag shapes on the tailor tack line. Seam the darts. With the right sides together, seam along the curved edge.
2 Repeat for the lining (diagram 1).
3 Cut two, 36in [91cm] strips of background fabric 3½in [9cm] wide.
4 To make the handles, fold the strips lengthwise, tuck the petersham inside, and turn the edges in. Machine down either side close to the edge.
5 Turn in the top of the bag about 1½in [4cm] and tack in position.
6 Machine the handles to the bag firmly, 4½in [11.5cm] from the side seams (diagram 2).
7 Place the lining inside and slip stitch in position (diagram 3).

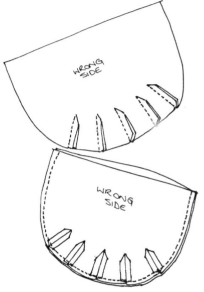

Diagram 1 Seam the darts and with right sides together seam along the curved edge for both the bag material and the lining

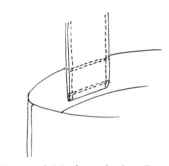

Diagram 2 Machine the handles to the bag

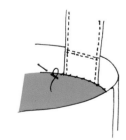

Diagram 3 Place the lining inside the bag and slip stitch into position

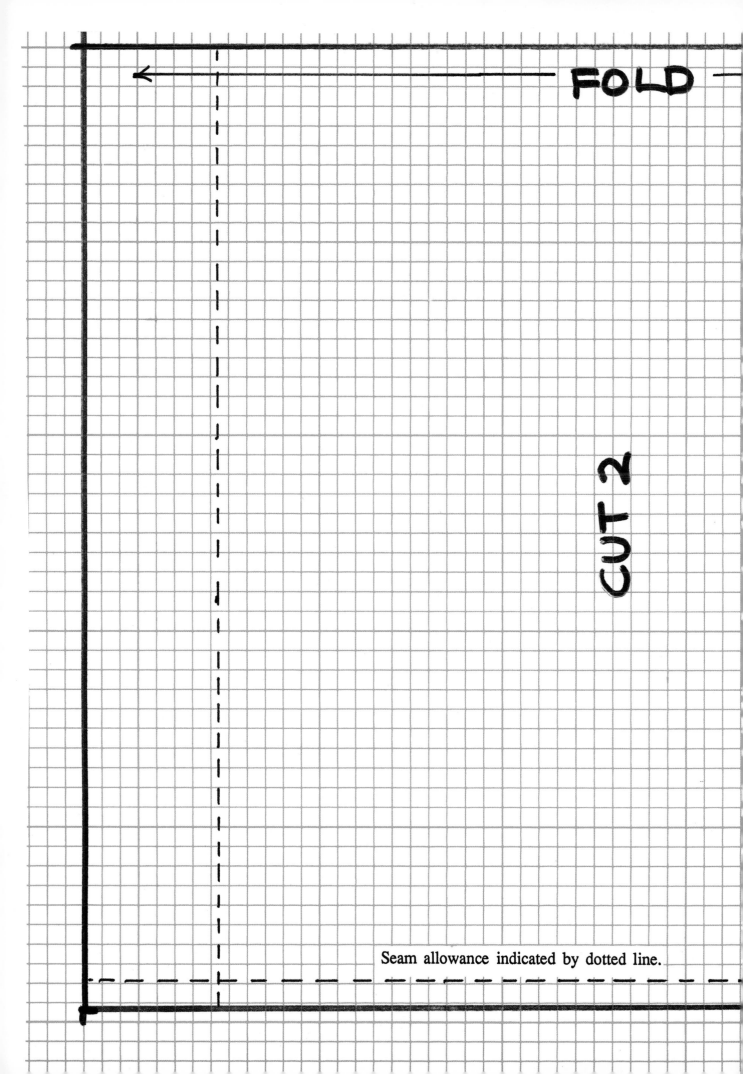

FOLD

CUT 2

Seam allowance indicated by dotted line.

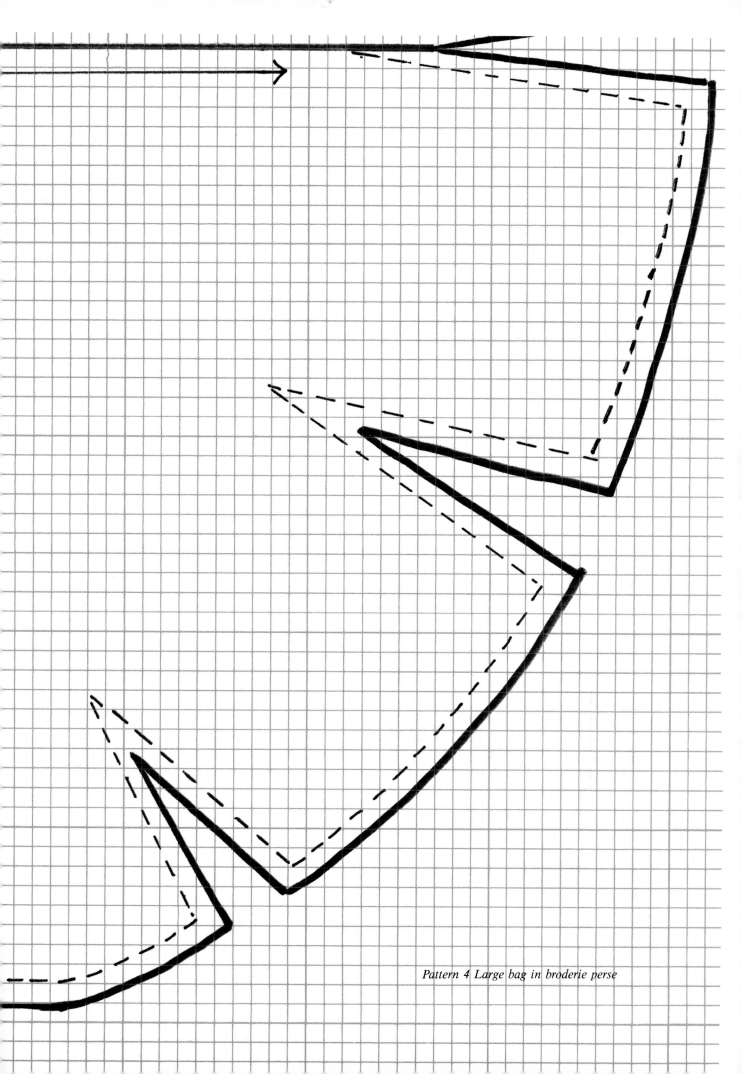

Pattern 4 Large bag in broderie perse

PINCUSHION in layered appliqué

There are several kinds of layered appliqué, as fabrics can be applied to the back as well as the front of the material. When a piece is applied to the back and then the top layer cut away to reveal it, the technique is called reverse appliqué. In the case of the pincushion, three layers have been combined so that two can be cut away.

Materials

2 × 6in [15cm] squares of jade felt.
1 × 6in [15cm] square of cerise felt.
1 × 6in [15cm] square of royal blue satin.
Dark blue and cerise sewing thread.

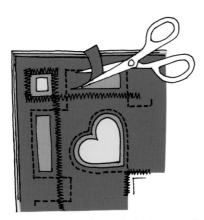

Diagram 1 Cut through the layers of coloured felt to reveal the satin layer

Directions

1 Mark the design on one of the jade felt pieces.
2 Lay the satin on a flat surface, put the cerise felt on top of it, and the jade felt on top of it again. Tack together through all layers.
3 Machine a narrow satin stitch around the small centre square, the large outer square, and corner squares, in dark blue thread. Straight stitch around all the other outlines, in cerise.
4 Cut away to the cerise layer, about ⅛in [3mm] from the machining, in the areas as shown in the photograph.
5 Cut through the pink layer to reveal the satin (diagram 1).

Making up

1 Put the remaining piece of jade felt back to back with the embroidery, and machine straight stitch around the edge twice, about ⅛in [3mm] in from the edge.
2 Slit the felt back down the centre, insert a pad, and sew up the slit by hand. The pad is a 'bag' made from any fabric and filled with cleaned fleece. The oil in the fleece will stop needles rusting.

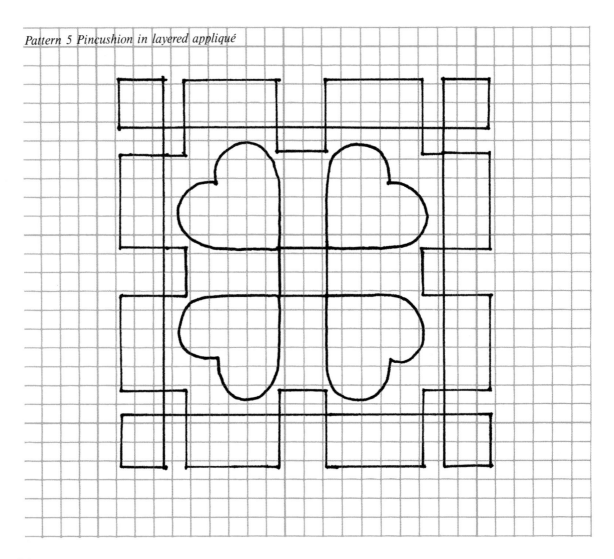

Pattern 5 Pincushion in layered appliqué

CUTWORK

In the shops today there are many examples of machine cutwork done on multiple head machines in a repetitive way, on clothing for example. But there is still a place for individually worked cutwork on the domestic machine. The handkerchief example illustrates the basic technique, but there are variations that can be developed, and suggestions are given afterwards.

CUTWORK HANDKERCHIEF

Materials

12in [30cm] square of lawn.
Rayon machine embroidery thread to match [Madeira or Natesh].

Pattern 6 Cutwork handkerchief

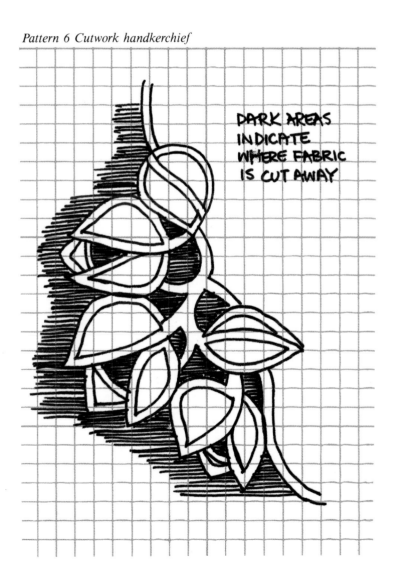

37

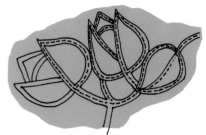

Diagram 1 Machine straight stitch between the double traced lines

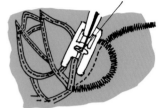

Diagram 2 Machine over the straight stitch with satin stitch

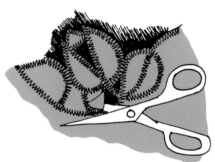

Diagram 3 Cut out the areas indicated on the pattern

Directions

1 Trace the design onto a corner of the lawn, ½in [1.2cm] from the edge. Machine a short straight stitch between the double lines. This acts as stay stitching (diagram 1).
2 Set the machine to a medium width satin stitch and machine over the straight stitch. Try to work out a sequence with as few stops and starts as possible, and make sure all ends are secure (diagram 2).
3 Press the embroidery from the wrong side with a damp cloth.
4 Cut out areas indicated with very sharp scissors. It is often easier to cut from the back pulling the material back and tensioning it, to prevent cutting the stitchery (diagram 3).
5 To finish 'hemming' the rest of the handkerchief, turn the raw edges of the material under a full ¼in [6mm] and machine straight stitch as near the edge as possible. Trim the fabric as close to the stitching as possible.
6 Turn this edge under, and zigzag over it using a narrow, close zigzag, but not satin stitch which will 'stick'.

This same design can be used in a variety of ways, by repeating it as shown (diagram 4), and by enlarging it. The design could be applied to such items as collars, pockets, neck or sleeve edges, etc.

A slight variation of the technique is to apply iron-on interfacing to a fabric, and cut out after the straight stitching and before the satin stitch. This makes the cutting out easier.

Instead of using the same width of zigzag throughout, vary it; for example, the flowers could be in wider satin stitch than the stems and leaves. In 'free' machining, described later in the book (p.74), the width can be altered within one shape while stitching is in progress.

Multicoloured thread can be used giving blocks of one colour and then another. If the blocks of colour are too strong, instead of working one row of satin stitch, work one row of a slightly open zigzag on top of the other, which will have the effect of blending the colours.

Diagram 4 The design can be varied by repeating or enlarging it

TUFTING

This is one of the easiest effects to achieve. For it you will need a firm fabric, such as calico, sailcloth, or a closely woven furnishing fabric. You will also need a U-shaped tool in metal. This can be a tool sold specifically for the purpose, a hairpin crochet tool, or a piece cut from a wire coat hanger (diagram 1). The yarn can be any thread, but a remnant of knitting yarn is probably the most convenient to begin with.

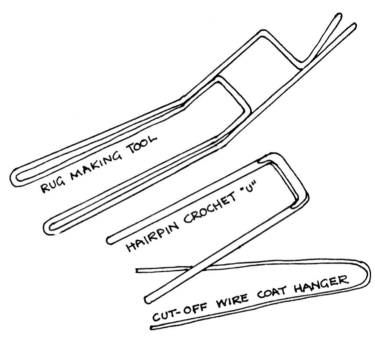

Diagram 1 Tools which can be used for tufting

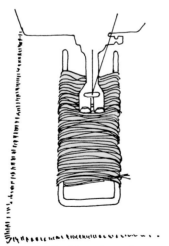

Diagram 2 Machine along the centre of the wound thread

Mark a line on the fabric with a soluble marker or dress maker's chalk. Wind the yarn round the U-shaped tool, along its full length. If the winding is very close together, the tufting will be thick, and if thinly wound, it will be sparse.

Select an ordinary sewing thread that matches the colour of the yarn to thread the machine both top and bottom.

Set the machine to a short ¹⁄₁₆in [1.5mm] straight stitch. Place the foot in the centre of the wound thread and machine along its length, gradually easing out the U-shaped tool at the same time (diagram 2). If it is a decorative piece, one line of machining is sufficient, but if it is to be practical, machine back along the first line of stitching. There is now a choice between cutting the loops, or leaving them (diagram 3).

If an area of tufting is required, work successive rows close together ½in [1.2cm] apart. This means pushing the previous row to one side as the next row is stitched, or the tufting will look ridged (diagram 4).

Colours can be easily mixed in this technique. When winding onto the U-shaped tool, take the ends from three or more balls or reels of thread and wind them simultaneously. The threads need not be all of the same thickness or texture. For example, metal threads can be combined with synthetic or wool.

To produce a shaded effect, start with three pale colours, for example, white, cream and pale pink, and wind six times. Cut the white and introduce beige for six more winds. Then introduce yellow instead of the cream, and so on, gradually introducing darker threads and cutting out the paler ones.

Instead of yarn, strips of fabric may be used for a chunkier effect. When worked on a firm hessian [burlap] backing, rugs can be readily made in far less time than hand techniques and yet still remain individual in colour selection and design. The fabric need not be new, as discarded clothing can well be recycled. It need not be only plain coloured, as patterned fabric cut in strips gives quite a different effect to the original pattern.

Colour does need to be controlled though, and if it is not possible to find fabrics with a common colour link, dunk a collection of fabrics in a dye bath. They will come out in a range of tones and variations of the original colour, but will be linked pleasingly. Experiments can be made by cutting the fabric on the straight or on the cross, to give different pattern or textural effects.

As the machine will need to go through thick layering, use a sturdy needle, size 100, and an ordinary sewing thread.

Diagram 3 The loops can be cut or left intact

Diagram 4 Close up the previous row and push to one side as the next tow is stitched

CUSHION

Materials

½yd [46cm] of cotton twill or similar.

Cushion pad 16in [40cm] square.

Yarns in the following colours — cream, pale green, pale yellow, yellow, cinnamon, orange, pink, red.

The yarns in the cushion shown in the photograph are equivalent to a 4ply knitting yarn, about 1oz [30gram] of each colour.

Ordinary yellow sewing thread to match the material.

A U-shaped tool with prongs 1½in [4cm] apart.

Directions

1 Cut the material in half, i.e. two 18in [46cm] squares.
2 Mark the design on one square of fabric with a fabric marker or tailor's chalk. The design given is a quarter of the design so it is repeated four times.
3 Grading the colour as described in the general instructions for tufting, work the four centre lines first.
4 Then work the shorter lines, trimming off the 'corners' to form rounded shapes.

Diagram 1 The tufted square is marked with a line around the outer edge for sewing

42

Making up

1 Cut the other square in half. Make a narrow hem on one long side of each piece. Put the two hemmed edges together, one overlapping the other by about ¼in [6mm]. This will form the opening in the backing.

2 On the tufted square, mark a 15½in [39cm] outer line. Pin on the backing, wrong sides together, and machine on this line (diagram 1).

3 Trim the turning, on the backing only, to ¼in [6mm]. Turn the front edge over and hem on the machine line by hand (diagram 2).

4 Insert the pad and sew up the opening by hand.

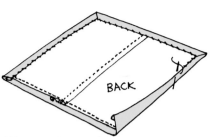

Diagram 2 Turn the front edge over and hem along the machine line

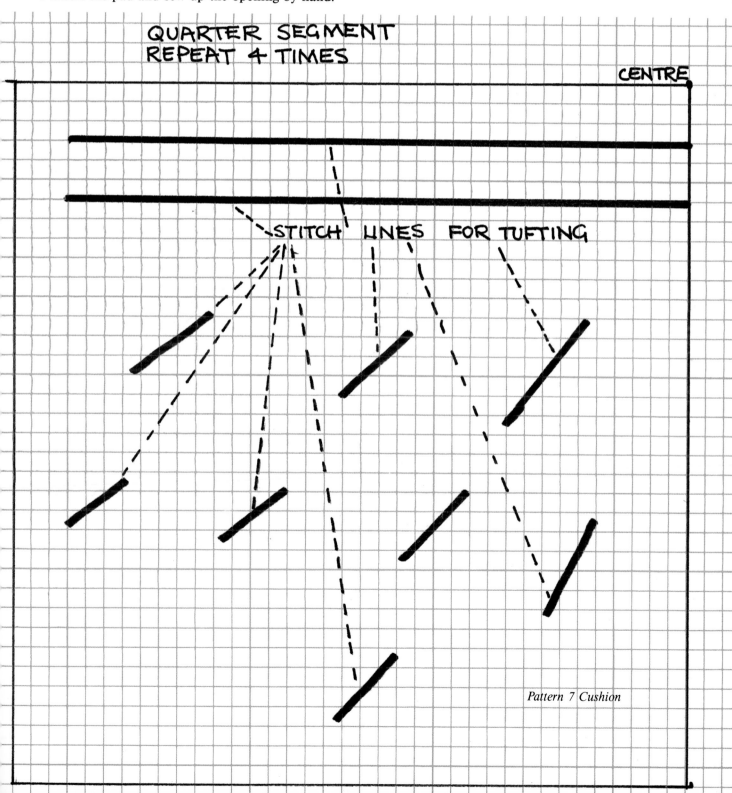

QUARTER SEGMENT
REPEAT 4 TIMES

CENTRE

STITCH LINES FOR TUFTING

Pattern 7 Cushion

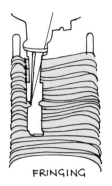

FRINGING

Diagram 1 To make a fringe, sew down the looped yarn on one side, close to the edge of the U-shaped tool

Fringing

This is the same technique as for tufting, except that instead of sewing down the centre of the U-shaped tool, sew as near to one side as possible (diagram 1). To make this easier, use the zipper foot. Let the foot lean against the U-shaped tool whilst machining. This will sew down the looped yarn on one side. Remove the U-shaped tool, and the fringe may be left looped, or cut on the edge opposite the machining. As an extra decoration, the heading of the fringe may be machined over with a pattern.

Any yarn may be used for fringing, but it is essential to wind the U-shaped tool evenly for a formal fringe.

FRINGED SCARF

Materials

Georgette, chiffon, or similar 54in × 10in [137cm × 25cm], cream or pale yellow.

Machine embroidery threads as follows — yellow Empress floss; silver and gold Astro Madeira; pink/salmon shaded, mauve/white shaded and bright yellow shiny rayon; Titania or Madeira. These threads are wound together onto the U-shaped tool to form the fringes.

Cream sewing thread to sew down the fringe.

A U-shaped tool with prongs 1½in [4cm] apart.

Directions

1 Begin by 'hemming' the edges of the scarf. Turn in a very narrow hem ¼in [6mm], and sew it down with a short straight stitch. Turn the hem again, and zigzag over the edge with a narrow zigzag, which will take in all the raw edges. In the scarf shown in the photograph, the ends were cut diagonally before being edged in the way described.
2 Trace on the lines with a dissolvable pen, and machine the fringing on the lines.
3 To obtain the shaggy effect, cut the fringing three different lengths; some threads quite close to the stitching, some halfway and some on the edge of the loop.

TAILOR TACK FEET

The vertical metal bar (shaded) creates looped stitches.

Diagram 1 The tailor tack foot has a metal ridge down the centre

Diagram 2 A line of looped thread will be created by the tailor tack foot

Tufting using the tailor tack foot

The tailor tack foot has a ridge down the centre (diagram 1). The machine must always be set to zigzag when using the tailor tack foot, or the needle will hit the ridge and break. For decorative purposes, set the machine to the narrowest zigzag feasible, and a very short stitch length. Thread the machine as normal and start machining; a ridge of looped thread will gradually emerge (diagram 2). Depending on the thread being used, it may be necessary to slacken the top tension minimally. It is not advisable to cut the loops, as the bobbin thread is not sufficient to hold the loops in place. However, succeeding rows may be worked to fill an area.

Experiment by machining a succession of rows in differing threads. The bobbin thread need not be changed each time, only the top thread. Ordinary sewing threads can contrast with shiny rayon threads, or metallic ones. Multicoloured threads will make blocks of colour in succession.

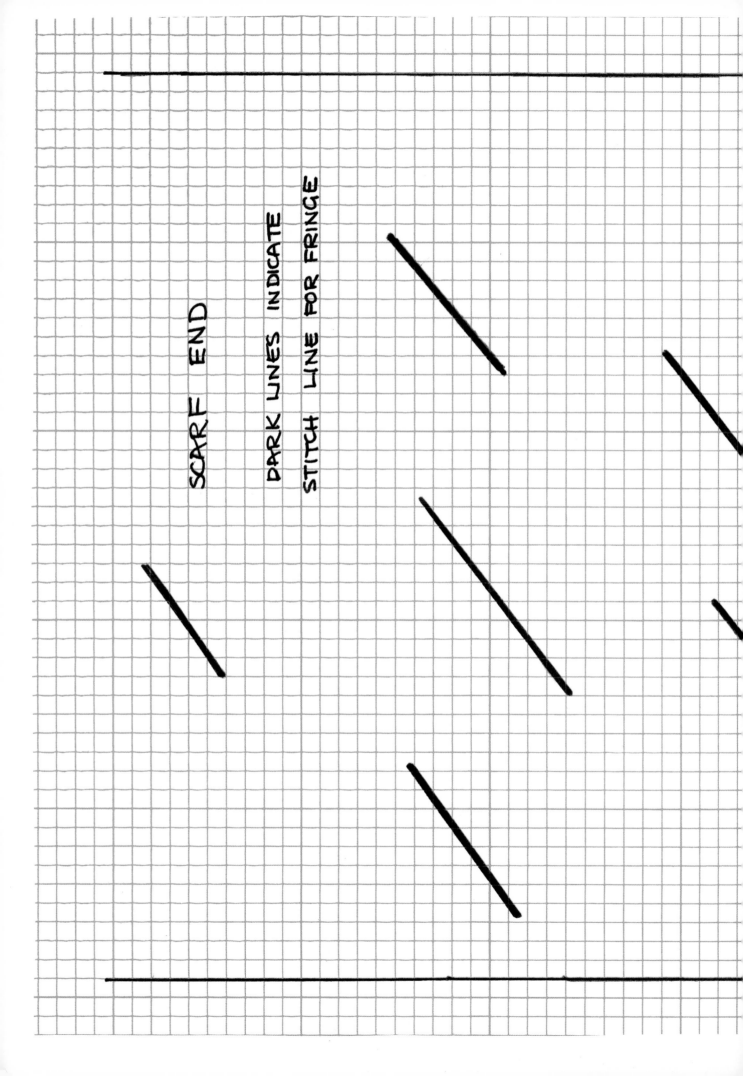

SCARF END

DARK LINES INDICATE

STITCH LINE FOR FRINGE

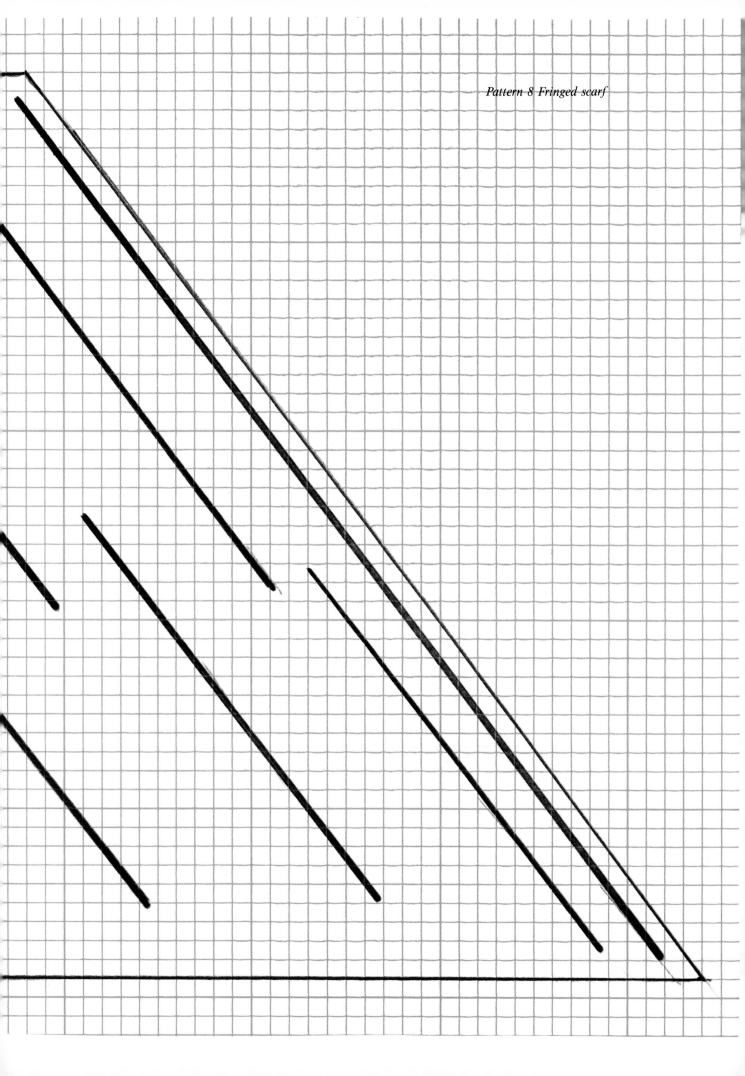

Pattern 8 Fringed scarf

BOW

Materials

6in × 14in [15cm × 36cm] of fine, closely woven material such as shantung, or a light dress-weight polyester.

Threads — Madeira Astro, gold and multicoloured. Ordinary sewing cotton to match fabric.

Directions

1 First make up the bow. Put the right sides together and machine on the seam line, leaving one end open. Snip the seam on the curves to allow the material to stretch (diagram 1). Turn through to the right side. Turn in the end and slip stitch to close the seam. Press.

Diagram 1 Snip the material at the edge of the curves to allow for stretching

2 Trace the design on the fabric. Tailor tack the three outer lines with the multicoloured Astro. Set the machine to a narrow, close zigzag, and machine the other lines in gold, including a line at either end of the bow, ¹⁄₁₆in [1.5mm] in from the edge.

3 Put the ends of the bow together, right sides outside, and straight stitch two lines across the narrowest part, with ordinary sewing thread (diagram 2).

4 Open the bow out to the final shape, and catch stitch the bow in place at the centre (diagram 3).

The finished bow can be sewn to a hair slide or comb as a hair decoration, or to a piece of elastic for a bow tie, or attached to the front of court shoes to make them special. Several bows could form rich decoration down the front of a tunic top, or spaced down a sleeve.

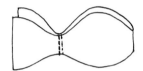

Diagram 2 With right sides outside, stitch two lines across the narrowest part

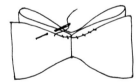

Diagram 3 Open the bow out to the final shape and catch stitch at the centre

Pattern 9 Bow

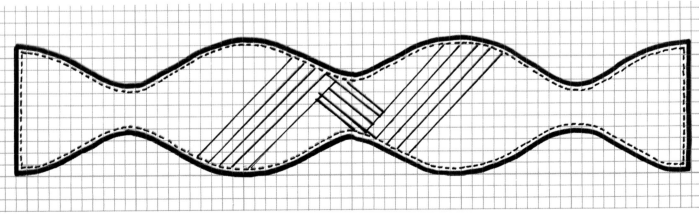

QUILTING

Quilting is a very familiar form of fabric decoration as it can be seen on garments of all kinds, because it is both practical and attractive to look at. Besides clothing, quilting makes cushions look more luxurious, and adds warmth and pattern to quilts. This familiar sort of quilting is invariably made of three layers, a top layer, wadding or batting, and a backing, which are held together by lines of stitching. It is usually known as English quilting, however there are other kinds of quilting that will be described later.

The main problem in producing an attractive piece of quilting, is to ensure that all three layers are sewn together evenly, without wrinkling. This is more difficult by machine than by hand as the machine foot tends to push the fabric ahead of it, and not all three layers at the same pace. However, there are now two techniques to prevent this.

The first of these is the 'walking foot'; this either comes as part of the machine, or as an added accessory. The teeth, or feed, pushes the material from the underside. The purpose of the walking foot is to feed the top layer of fabric through at the same pace, thereby preventing 'slip'. It is used in conjunction with the ordinary sewing foot, unless otherwise instructed by the maker (diagram 1).

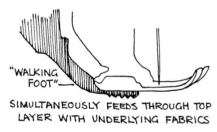

SIMULTANEOUSLY FEEDS THROUGH TOP LAYER WITH UNDERLYING FABRICS

Diagram 1 The use of the walking foot in quilting enables the layers of material to feed through the machine evenly

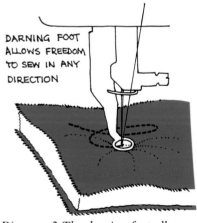

DARNING FOOT ALLOWS FREEDOM TO SEW IN ANY DIRECTION

Diagram 2 The darning foot allows more freedom of movement

The other option is to use the darning foot, with the teeth down. However this will only work where the darning foot bobs up and down with each stitch, on such makes as Bernina, Elna and Pfaff, or otherwise the fabric jams, unless a very thin batting is used. When it is possible to use this technique it means that there is much more freedom of movement as the fabric can be moved in any direction, allowing very small or intricate shapes to be sewn (diagram 2).

One very important point to remember is that quilting can 'shrink' the materials; so either leave very generous turnings, or do not cut out the clothing pieces until the quilting is completed.

The sort of materials which show quilting off to best effect have a smooth surface and are pale in colour. This is because quilting shows to fullest effect when the shadow cast by the indentations can be seen most clearly. For the same reason, a fabric that has a gloss or sheen is even more effective. To mould well into the hills and valleys of quilting, a fabric must also be supple, so avoid stiff materials. Amongst the most suitable fabrics are thin cottons, polycottons, soft pure silks, lightweight synthetic or pure silk satins and fine wools.

As regards threads, probably ordinary sewing thread is the most reliable to machine quilt with, though rayon and metallic threads can enliven the effect. In general, use a colour that is very near that of the fabric, or the sewn line can dominate the quilting.

General instructions for machining English quilting

1 Iron the top layer and backing because, once they are quilted, it will be too late!
2 On a flat surface, lay the top layer face down, place down the batting and then the backing. Smooth each layer as it is put down to make sure there are no wrinkles.
3 Pin the work all over from the back, starting from the middle and working outwards (diagram 3).

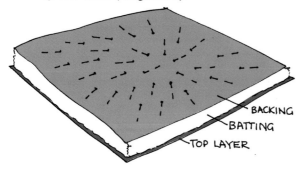

Diagram 3 Pin the quilting layers together from the back

4 Turn onto the right side and begin machining, employing either of the techniques already mentioned. **Always** work from the centre outwards to spread the layers out evenly. Re-arrange the pins if the fabrics begin to bunch, and in any case, remove them as the work progresses. Remember that besides straight stitch, it is also possible to use zigzag and patterns.

Batting or wadding

Either name may be correctly used, and there are a range of them available. The most commonly used batting nowadays, because it is washable, is synthetic, and it is sold by weight; the lighter the weight the thinner the batting. There is also cotton wadding, which normally has a papery outside. Although it is washable, it does compact down when washed, so is not suitable for anything frequently washed. Domette is another form of batting, and can either be cotton or wool. Cotton domette is a woven fabric, something like flanelette. Woolen domette is a fluffy knitted fabric and is warm without being bulky. Both domettes will wash with care, but are best not used for anything requiring frequent washing.

QUILTED CUSHION WITH A BUTTERFLY DESIGN

Materials

A pillow pad.
2 pieces of fabric the size of the pillow plus 4in [10cm] extra
   both ways.
Sewing thread the same colour as the fabric.
Batting a little bigger than the pillow.
Backing, same size as batting.
Pencil and paper.

Directions

1 Trace the butterfly and cut it out of paper 8 times.
2 Lay the top fabric flat on a smooth surface.
3 Arrange the paper butterflies on the fabric in a pattern and
   pin in place. Remember to leave sufficient room at the edge
   for making up.
4 Draw round the paper butterflies with a dissolvable pen or
   dressmaker's pencil; mark lines for any patterning. Remove
   pins and paper butterflies.

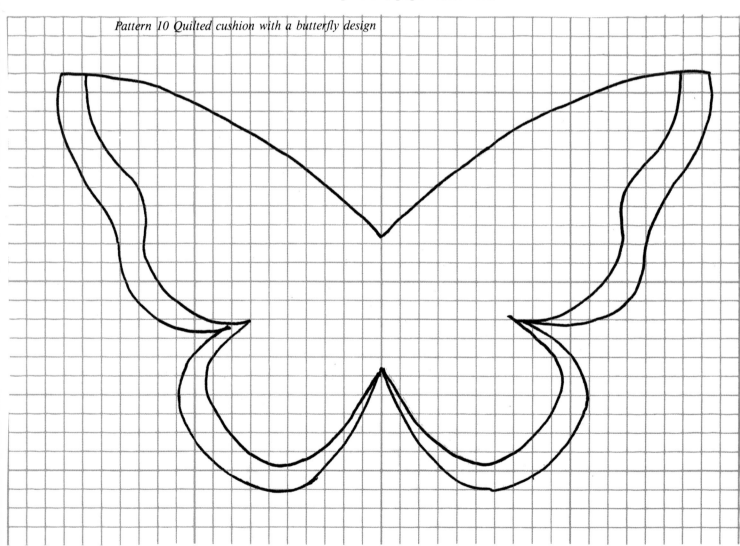

Pattern 10 Quilted cushion with a butterfly design

5 Follow the directions for English quilting. Each butterfly can be worked with a different outline stitch or pattern, or straight stitch and zigzag.

6 Make up the cushion as given in the directions on p 43. After sewing the front to the back, trim away the batting and the backing close to the line of machine stitching, then carry on.

Note that a cushion cover needs to be about ½in [1.2cm] smaller than its pad to look nice and plump when it is finished.

3-DIMENSIONAL FLOWER in English quilting

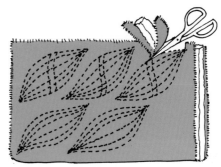

Materials

Fabric [satin] about 18in [46cm] square.
Sewing thread to match.
2oz [56.5gram] batting 18in × 9in [46cm × 23cm].

Directions

1 Trace the leaf shape in Pattern 11 and cut 5 paper shapes of it.
2 Lay the fabric on a flat surface and pin the paper shapes on half of it, as close together as is practical.
3 Mark around the leaf shapes and on 3 also mark the centre line. Remove paper shapes and pins.
4 Put batting underneath the marked area and fold the rest of the material under it.
5 English quilt the 5 leaf shapes following the general instructions for machining English quilting. Firstly sew around the outline of the leaf shapes and then sew four lines randomly down the length, all in straight stitch. On 3 leaves also sew two lines either side of the marked centre line (diagram 1).
6 Cut out the leaves close to the stitching at the edge, and cut the 3 leaves in half between the two centre lines of stitching.
7 Zigzag around the edge to cover the raw edges; this will make the shapes twist. If the first line of stitching does not cover, simply go over it again. The zigzag should be set to about ³⁄₁₆in [5mm] width and as short as possible in length. Finish off the ends by darning them in (diagram 2).
8 By hand, sew the half leaves together (diagram 3), one on top of another, in a spiral arrangement to make a flower, and back with the two leaves to make a corsage. This in turn can be sewn to a brooch mount or a hairslide, or clip.

In fact these simple shapes can be arranged in a variety of ways, as can be seen in the photograph.

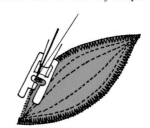

Diagram 1 Sew around the outline of the leaves, lengthways down them and across the centre on three of the leaves and then cut out the leaf shapes

Diagram 2 Zigzag around the edge of the leaf

Diagram 3 Sew the half leaves together in a spiral arrangement

Pattern 11 3-dimensional flower in English quilting

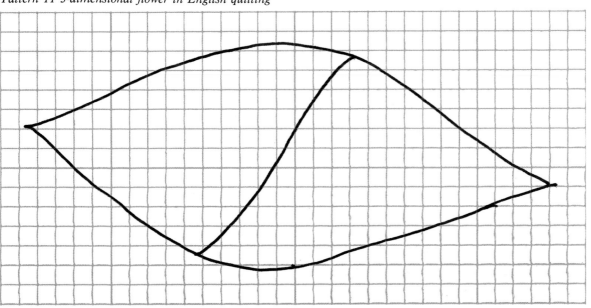

COT OR PRAM COVER in English quilting

This design is based on a traditional form of pattern making for quilting. One shape of template is repeated in different positions to form patterns for borders, motifs and overall designs. This small cover only shows a border and a simple centre motif, based on the repetition of a heart template; but from this one shape many more permutations of pattern can be invented.

The cot cover is reversible, having one colour one side and another on the back. By using washable fabrics and batting it is very practical.

Materials

½yd [46cm] of pink polycotton in pink.
½yd [46cm] of off-white polycotton.
½yd [46cm] lightweight batting.
Off-white synthetic sewing thread.
1yd [91cm] off-white narrow ribbon.

Directions

1 Plan the design on paper within a 13in × 17in [33cm × 43cm] oblong. Find the centre by folding the paper in half both ways. Also fold it cornerwise. This will mark the centre and corner of the border, and the placing of the central motif. Cut 22 heart shapes from paper and arrange in the pattern as illustrated in the photograph and in diagram 1. Draw around them. Now you have a record of the design. The little shapes in between can be drawn free hand as they echo the heart shapes outline (diagram 1).

Diagram 1 Position the heart shapes using the fold lines as a guide to balance the design

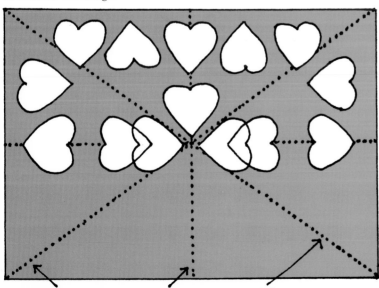

FOLDS ACT AS GUIDE LINES

2 Using the same templates and the same system, mark the design on the fabric with a dissolvable pen or dressmaker's pencil.

3 Layer the batting and two layers of fabric ready for English quilting. Remember to work from the centre outwards. Machine the whole design in straight stitch first. Then emphasise the central motif, and every other heart in the border by working a narrow, fairly close zigzag over the straight stitch.

4 Work two rows of satin stitch scalloping down the sides, ½in [1.2cm] away from the quilting.

5 Straight stitch along the ends 1in [2.5cm] from the quilting and then machine two lines of satin stitch close together, ⅛in [3mm] beyond that.

6 Trim off the fabric close to the stitching.

7 Add small ribbon bows at the centre and corners.

Pattern 12 Cot or pram cover in English quilting

SMALL BAG in English quilting

This uses machining to flatten out the background, so that the flower motifs stand out in relief.

Materials

½yd [46cm] pure silk or similar.
2oz [56.5gram] batting approximately 18in × 8in [46cm × 20cm].
1 reel multicoloured rayon thread. In the example shown in the photograph the material is pale green and the thread a blue/pink/green/yellow mixture.
Backing; thin calico or polycotton.

Directions

1 Trace two flowers and part of a flower outline in black felt tip pen on white paper, arranging them in the positions shown in diagram 1.
2 Cut a piece of silk 8in × 10in [20cm × 25cm]. Place the design underneath it and trace the outline onto the fabric, with a dissolvable pen or similar.

Diagram 1 Trace the flower and the outline of half the flower

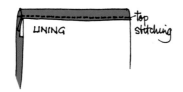

Diagram 2 Sew the lining to the top edge of the quilting and top stitch in position

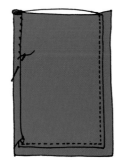

Diagram 3 Turn over the top layer of the front to make a mock binding and hem

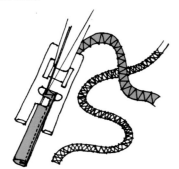

Diagram 4 Zigzag twice over the strips of material being used for the straps

3 Layer this piece, half the batting and the backing, and quilt with straight stitch along the main lines of the design.
4 Work lines of straight stitch close together in the background to flatten it, about 1/10in [2mm] apart. Allow the rows to end in a random fashion.
5 If desired, a single flower can be repeated on the back.

Making up

1 Sew the lining to the top edge of the quilting, and fold over. Top stitch to hold in position and trim away the bulk from the seam. Repeat for back (diagram 2).
2 Place the front and back, wrong sides together, and pin carefully. Machine around the three raw edges 1in [2.5cm] from the edge. Sew a second line 1/10in [2mm] outside the first one.
3 Trim away the turning close to the stitching, **except** the top layer of the front.
4 Make a mock binding by turning this edge over the seam, covering all the raw edges and hem in position (diagram 3).
5 To make the straps, cut three pieces of material the full width of the fabric and 1 1/2in [4cm] wide. Turn in the edges and machine in place. Set the zigzag as wide as possible, and fairly long, and zigzag over these strips. It may be necessary to do this twice, to enclose all the fabric with the stitching (diagram 4). Lightly plait the three strips together, loop the ends and oversew to the bag at either side.

This same design could be used on larger articles, such as a cushion, by repeating the design several times, or on a pin cushion by quilting just one flower.

Pattern 13 Small bag in English quilting

Twin needle Italian or corded quilting

The twin needle is just what its name suggests, two needles in one shank. It is inserted in the machine like any other needle (diagram 1). Two reels of thread are needed and are threaded through the tension checks and guides in the same way as a single thread. If there is a choice, thread one thread to one side of the tension disc, and one to the other. This is usually possible on modern machines, but may not be on older ones. Twin needles can be bought in several different spacings, for very fine tucks or bolder tucks. Each width of twin needle has a matching special foot to allow parallel rows of twin needle stitch to be worked easily. It is not absolutely necessary to use the matching foot, as the ordinary sewing foot can be used, but will result in a less raised effect.

Machining with the twin needle in straight stitch closely resembles fine Italian quilting, that is, parallel lines of stitching which raise the fabric between them. If a bolder raised line is desired, a fine cord can be inserted at the time of stitching. This is usually fed through a hole in the plate, but as it varies from machine to machine, consult the machine manual.

It is difficult to believe that twin needles will work, but they do!

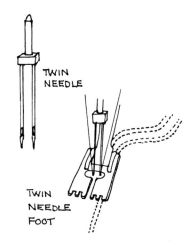

Diagram 1 The twin needle and twin needle foot can be attached on the machine easily following the manufacturer's instructions

JACKET with twin needle decoration

Materials

The materials are for a medium size 32in-37in bust [81cm-94cm].
2yd [1.8m] of lightweight suiting or flannel; minimum 62in [157cm] wide.
Ordinary sewing thread to match, 2 reels.
Spool of fine cord, if used.
Lining.
Two shoulder pads.

Directions

1 Mark the design on the fabric. Do not cut it out (diagram 1).
2 Work all the lines in twin needle making sure the ends are secure. The cord, if used, can be cut off close to the end of the stitching.
3 Machine satin stitch ½in [1.2cm] at the end of each line to give definition to the end of the line of stitching (diagram 2).

Making up

1 Cut out the jacket. Cut facings for the front edge and neck. Stay stitch the neck edge.
2 Seam the underarm, clipping on the curve. Oversew the seam edges.
3 Turn up the sleeve hem about 1in [2.5cm], tack and slip stitch.

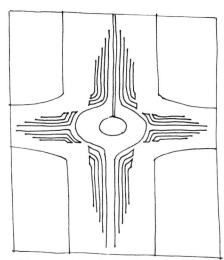

Diagram 1 Mark the design to be machined on the fabric

Diagram 2 Machine satin stitch at the end of each line of stitching

Pattern 14 Jacket

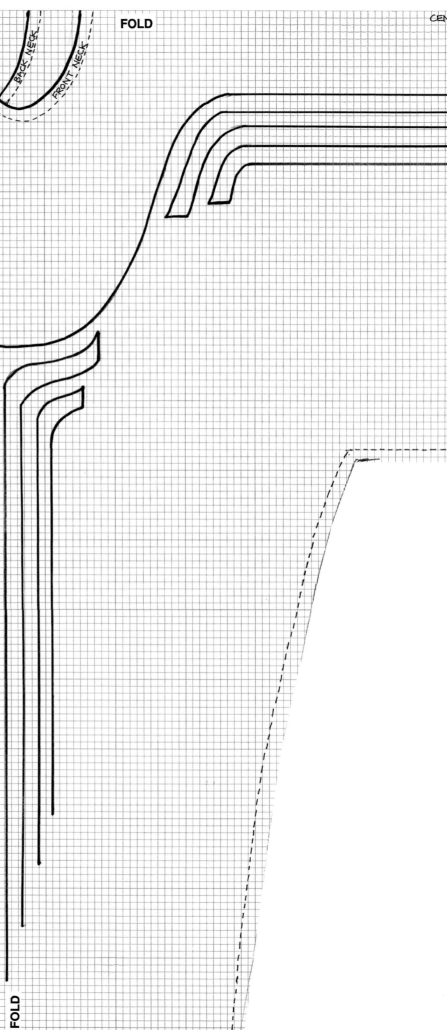

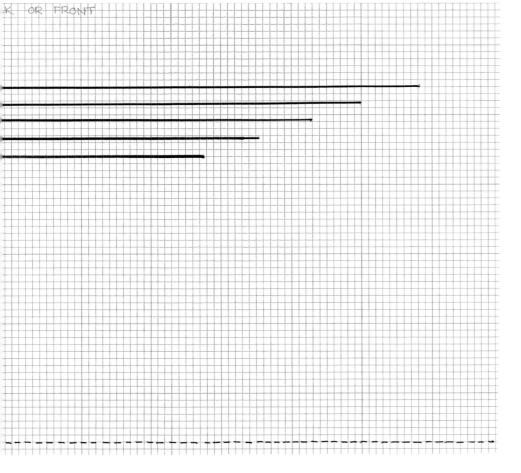

So that no joining of the embroidery is necessary, the jacket is made all in one piece.

4 Turn up the bottom hem to the desired length, tack and slip stitch.

5 Interline the facing. Face the neck and front edge, clipping at close intervals on the curves. Top stitch the neck and front edges.

6 Turn the jacket inside out. Attach shoulder pads to the neck facing and twin needling on the shoulder line (diagram 3).

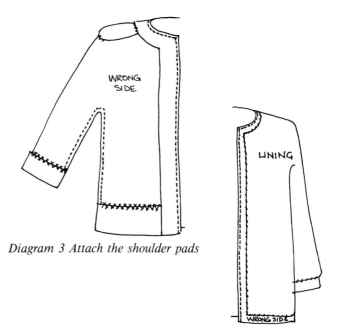

Diagram 3 Attach the shoulder pads

Diagram 4 Sew the lining into the jacket

7 Cut out the lining as for the jacket except shorter in length, and deeper in the neckline. Seam the underarm. With the jacket still inside out, sew in the lining by hand, first around the neck and front edges, then across the shoulder pads. Lastly attach around the sleeve and bottom hems, leaving plenty of 'give' (diagram 4).

Note that as an alternative to facing and lining the jacket, the edges could simply be bound with a bias strip.

Twin needle is used on the jacket in a very basic way, but it can be developed interestingly in some of the following ways:
Use contrast coloured thread instead of a match.
Use a dark thread and a light thread which will suggest a permanent shadow.
Try twin needle on transparent fabric, with a coloured cord.
Swirl the fabric in curves, or try interweaving arabesques which will manipulate it into ridges and valleys. This is not applicable to clothing, but lends itself to adventurous experiment for purely decorative work.

COUCHING BY MACHINE

Couching is sewing down a thick thread with a thin one. As really thick threads cannot be threaded through the machine this solves the problem where a bolder effect is desired. Thick yarns such as knitting and weaving threads can be sewn down with straight stitch, zigzag or patterns. The threads can be hand guided under the foot, but it can be difficult to get them straight (diagram 1). A useful aid to guiding the yarn can be the foot intended for turning hems. This has a small funnel shape into which the yarn can be fed so that it is led directly under the needle (diagram 2). This means that a straight stitch will sew it down exactly in the middle and it also centres the yarn for working zigzag or patterning over it (diagram 3). Fine ribbons or ribbon-like knitting yarns can be threaded and sewn in the same way.

Diagram 1 Thick threads can be guided by hand under the foot

Diagram 2 The hemming foot is a useful aid in keeping couching straight

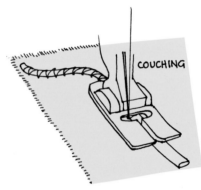

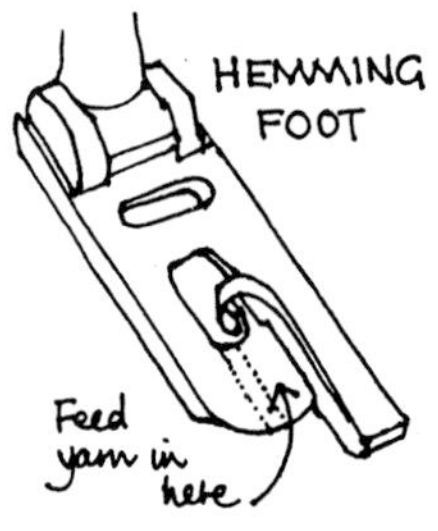

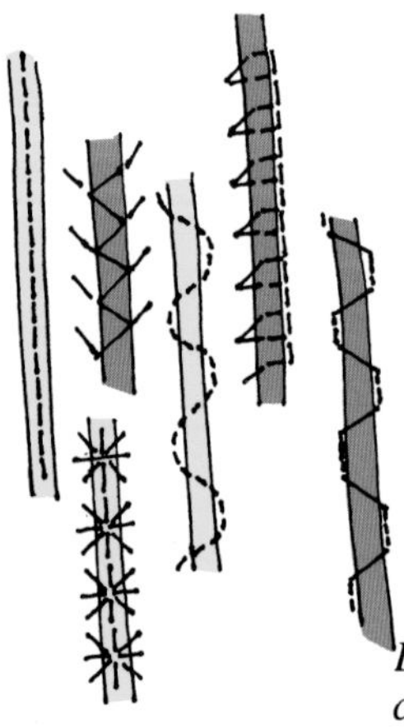

Diagram 3 A large variety of stitches can be used for couching

BELT decorated with couched threads and ribbon

Materials

Petersham or firm ribbon 1 ½in [4cm] wide and twice the waist
    measurement plus 3in [7.5cm]; in black.
Thick knitting yarn; about 6yd [5.5m] in red, plum, maroon,
    dark brown.
1yd [91cm] of gold ribbon ⅛in [3mm] wide.
1yd [91cm] of gold knitting yarn.
Black sewing cotton.
Gold machine thread, e.g. Madeira Astro.
1 ½in [4cm] of black velcro or similar.

Directions

1 Fold the ribbon in half and bond together with bondaweb;
    this is to strengthen the ribbon.
2 Take three generous lengths of brown knitting yarn and pull
    the ends through the guide, allowing at least 4in [10cm] to
    overhang at the start. Machine it along one edge of the
    petersham with a stretch stitch, in black.
3 Butted up to it and in the same way, work a row of red yarn.
    Then thinner rows of gold and plum.
4 Starting along the outer edge, and in the same way, machine
    rows of maroon, then red, then gold ribbon.
5 Machine a narrow, open zigzag of gold thread over the edge
    of the maroon yarn, and stretch stitch over the gold knitting
    yarn.
6 Make the dangling ends into tassels by winding or wrapping
    with black thread to make a 'head'. Before doing this the
    tassels can be filled out with added black thread.
7 Sew velcro on the underside of the tasselled end and on top
    of the other end.

Successive rows of couching can 'shrink' the material they are
sewn on to, so allow for this by being generous with the length.

    All sorts of different effects can be achieved depending on the
stitch used to sew the yarns down. Using contrasting colours,
for example red stitching on top of a blue yarn, could give an
overall purple tinge. By machining a bold pattern on top of
contrasting coloured yarns, a braid like effect would result. A
very rich raised line can be made by working several layers of
satin stitch over string.

MACHINING ON PLASTIC

Plastic is around us in everyday life, and yet we despise it as a base for embroidery. This is probably because it seems so transitory, which it is. However it has other useful qualities such as being totally transparent, and non-fraying and it usually costs very little. It is a fun material to use if its qualities are understood and accepted.

It is not possible to pin plastic, unless the pin marks can be made part of the design. So one of the most appropriate techniques is to sandwich bits of fabric or threads between two layers of plastic, and static will hold them in place until machine stitching is completed.

CLUTCH BAG WITH PLASTIC FLAP

Materials

Plastic sleeve A4 size, or any similar file size.
¼yd [23cm] of purple silky fabric.
Scraps of glittery and brightly coloured fabric. In the bag shown in the photograph, silver, pink, gold and bronze pieces were used together with white twinkly organza.
Stiff interlining, such as pelmet vilene, 7½in × 9in [19cm × 23cm].
Silver machine embroidery thread, such as Madeira Astro.
Ordinary sewing thread to match purple fabric.

Directions

1 Trim off the sides of the sleeve so that the top can be peeled back, and the width is 7½in [19cm]. Trim the length to 9in [23cm].
2 Cut circles from the scraps of fabric in different sizes, 1in, ¾in and ½in [2.5cm, 2cm and 1.2cm]. Coins can make good templates for these sizes. Although they may not all be needed, cut about 20 of each size.
3 Place the circles between the layers of plastic and arrange them within the flap size which is 4½in × 7½in [11.5cm × 19cm]. The arrangement of the circles is random, just moving them about until it looks right. With the side of the hand, just smooth the two layers of plastic together, and the circles will be trapped.
4 Machine around the flap shape with straight stitch, about ⅛in [3mm] from the edge. Machine diagonal lines ¾in [2cm] apart, to hold the circles of material in place. Mark the first one with a water dissolvable pen, and thereafter use the foot as a gauge (diagram 1).
5 Machine a narrow open zigzag around the edge of the flap on top of the straight stitch.

Diagram 1 Machine diagonal lines of straight stitch to hold the material in position

Making up

1 Using the purple material, make a fabric bag 8½in × 9in [21cm × 23cm] leaving one side open. Turn in the open side. Machine straight stitch ½in [1.2cm] from the 9in [23cm] edges; this will form the gusset (diagram 2).
2 Slip the interlining into the 'pocket'. Slip stitch the opening.
3 Slip the ends of the plastic over this shape and machine along the edge of the plastic to attach it to the bag (diagram 3).
4 Fold the bag in half so that the gussets can be machined together on the wrong side. Then turn through to the right side and the bag is complete (diagram 4).

An entirely transparent bag can be made by retaining the whole plastic sleeve length and folding it in three. Machine down the sides and a pochette bag is made.

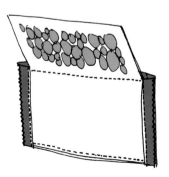

Diagram 2 Make a fabric bag to form the handbag gusset

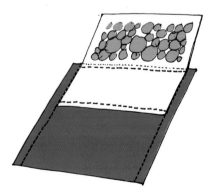

Diagram 3 Attach the plastic flap to the gusset

Diagram 4 Fold the gusset in half and machine together on the wrong side, then turn through to the right side

EARRINGS

Earrings can be made using the same sandwiching technique. Encapsulate pieces of fabric and/or thread snippets between two layers of plastic. Mark the shape of the earring, circle, square, or diamond for example, on the plastic. Machine straight stitch around the earring shape and cut out. Make a hole — a leather punch is ideal — to hang the earring on the mount.

A good source for larger pieces of plastic is the DIY hardware shop. The encapsulating technique can be the basis for blinds or hangings or banners. For this kind of piece the encapsulation could be developed with bolder opaque fabrics or other plastics including cut up shopping bags.

There is so much plastic available around us today, why not use it?

PICTURE MAKING

Sometimes it is fun to make a picture rather than an object, but where do you begin? Contrary to many people's belief, it is not possible to dream a good design out of the air; it has to be based on actuality which can be a photograph or a sketch. This provides a source of shapes and colours to choose from which are invariably much more interesting than anything relying solely on imagination. For most people a photograph is the most accessible reference; so, let's select a photograph.

If you are just beginning, choose a simple photograph without too much small detail, for example, one or two flowers rather than a whole flowerbed! You need not use the whole photograph. Cut two L shapes out of plain white paper, which can form a frame to help you select an area from the picture (diagram 1).

When picture making in fabric, it depends very much what there is in the fabric oddment bag, so there is no list of materials needed in this project. What follows is a system for picture making which can be applied to any photograph.

MARGUERITE PICTURE

Directions

1 Trace off only the main shapes. It is easier to do this if you use a paper that is not completely transparent, such as tissue paper. Use a felt tip pen rather than a pencil, so that there is no temptation to dither about and change; remember, trace only the main shapes. This can then be enlarged to the desired size.

2 Choose a background fabric. Look at the picture and decide what the main colour of the background is — it is rarely white! In the picture shown, a firm furnishing fabric in dark green, with indefinite stripes of brown and blue seemed the right tone and colour. Dark green is a good basis for many flowery subjects.

Diagram 1 Two L-shaped paper frames can be used to select an area of the photograph for the fabric design

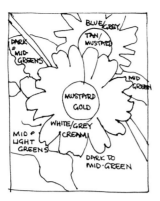

Diagram 2 Write the colours required in the picture on the tracing for reference

3 Now look at the rest of the picture to decide what other colours are needed and it is a good idea to write them on the tracing for reference (diagram 2). Try and rid yourself of preconceived ideas about the colours in the photograph. Although the flowers are white, within the flower there is also pale grey, pale blue and cream. By using mainly white, but combined with the other colours, the white will be emphasised and the flower will look alive and natural. In the same way the greens are not just one green but many. Gather together all the pieces of material, some of which can be very small. They can be any kind of material, from tweed to silk, in fact, the more varied the livelier the work. In general it is best to avoid patterned fabrics at this stage because they can dominate the whole design.

4 Iron the background fabric and lay it on a flat surface. Transfer the simple outline of the design onto the fabric.

5 Referring to the photograph and the notes, begin placing on pieces of fabric, about ½in [1.2cm] across. It is usually best to begin with the background shapes, in this case the green 'leaves'. The applied pieces can either be pinned or stuck in position. If sticking, use a fabric glue to avoid discolouring the material. Next the flowers; flower petals are never all the same shape or size. In the flower shown, three different petal shapes were used in four different kinds of fabric to make the design look more interesting.

6 When all the shapes are in position, the whole background is machined in an open zigzag in dark green thread, in a series of parallel lines. In the illustration the lines were worked diagonally. The white flower has been treated separately by sewing across the petals, in white, as the dark green would dull it too much.

Two things to bear in mind when working embroidered pictures are:
The medium is fabric and thread, not paint and pencil, so an impression is the aim, rather than fine botanical detail.
Although in general it is better to stick to the overall arrangement of shapes and colours in the photograph, you can alter the placing of small parts of the design. In the picture another flower was introduced in the top corner to balance the colour in the design.

FREE MACHINE EMBROIDERY

Although the main intention of this book is to introduce readers to the many alternatives of decoration that can be worked simply, with the machine in its normal sewing mode, the option of working 'freely' is much used nowadays, as it opens up a whole new range of possibilities.

To prepare a machine for free sewing, follow the darning instructions in the manual, which are:

Remove the foot — and put it somewhere safely.

Lower the feed, or teeth; or cover the feed with a plate supplied.

Set the stitch length to zero.

Always put the lever which operates the foot **down** when free machining even though the foot has been removed. This action is very easy to forget, and then you may wonder why the tension is doing strange things and producing long loops.

The fabric is mounted tightly in a round frame as the fabric must be quite flat on the machine bed (diagram 1).

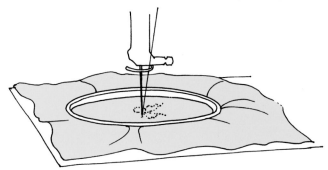

Diagram 1 Mount the fabric tightly in a round frame to keep it flat

To machine freely

Place the frame under the needle, holding it very lightly with both hands. Holding the top thread gently, take one stitch to bring the bobbin thread to the surface. Machine several stitches on the spot to fasten the threads, then cut close to the surface of the fabric.

Now the frame can be moved in any direction desired, up, down or sideways. The length of the stitch will be determined by the speed the frame is moved. Do not feel you have to hurry. Even when the machine appears to be running fast there is plenty of time, as the stitch will just be short. When experience and confidence have been gained with straight stitch, try some zigzag; simply set the zigzag to the required width and machine, still in any direction. All sorts of exciting effects can happen, quite by accident!

At this stage do not worry about tension. Free machine embroidery is a rare technique, because by doing it badly, the surface texture can be a most attractive mixture of loops in different colours!

There is sometimes a feeling that special threads are needed for free machine embroidery. The domestic sewing machine is designed to work with ordinary sewing threads, using the same kind of thread in both top and bobbin. When starting free machine embroidery, start with ordinary sewing thread. Then it is possible to move on to the delightful range of specialist threads with confidence later.

BRIDE'S HEADDRESS

The headdress was worked in free machine embroidery, but it could be worked with the foot on, but would take a bit longer. Butterflies were chosen for the design because they are a symbol of happiness.

Materials

¼yd [23cm] white organdie or organza. Organdie is cotton, organza is pure silk or synthetic; both are closely woven transparent fabrics.

Multicoloured rayon thread, palest pink, green, yellow, blue, e.g. Madeira or Natesh.

Silver thread, e.g. Madeira Astro.

1yd [91cm] of white flex, or wire that will mould easily.

4yd [3.6m] of white bias binding.

Pattern 15 Bride's headdress

Directions

1 Transfer 8 butterflies of each pattern shape onto the organdie, and 20 circles. Machine one kind of butterfly using silver thread in straight stitch along the design lines. Machine the other kind of butterfly, and all the circles, in the multicoloured thread in straight stitch along the design lines. Press the embroidery if necessary.
2 Cut them all out quite closely to the stitchery.
3 Fold all the butterflies in half and machine as near the fold line as possible; this makes their wings stand up (diagram 1).
4 Fold the circles in four and stitch across the corner; prise open to form a 'flower' (diagram 2).
5 Cut 6in [15cm] off the end of the flex. Wrap double sided tape over each end. Leaving a 6in [15cm] end, begin winding the bias binding around the flex. The double sided tape will hold it at the beginning and when the end is reached. Leave 6in [15cm] of bias binding over at the end (diagram 3).
6 Make a circle of half the covered flex and entwine the ends around it, leaving the bias ends as streamers. Oversew the flex ends together (diagram 4).

Diagram 1 Fold the butterfly shapes in half and stitch close to the fold line

Diagram 2 Fold the circles in four and stitch across the corner

Diagram 3 Wind the bias binding around the flex and leave a length of bias binding over at the end

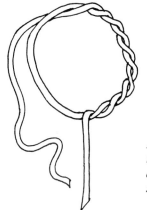

Diagram 4 Create a circle using half the covered flex and entwine the ends around it, leaving the bias ends as streamers

7 Machine zigzag over each end of bias binding two or three times. Use an open wide zigzag to enclose the binding.
8 Sew the flowers by hand onto the frame first, at about 1in [2.5cm] intervals. Sew the flowers onto to the side of the frame rather than the top (diagram 5). Then sew the butterflies on, at about 1½in [4cm] intervals.
9 Lastly sew the remaining butterflies and flowers down the streamers.

This technique of producing freestanding shapes from transparent fabric can, of course, be adapted to other design shapes of flowers and leaves, for example. The shapes could be grouped together to make a corsage, a picture, or a three dimensional embroidery of a pot of flowers. The fabric can be coloured with sponged-on paints or dyes, rather than being plain white. Any leftover shapes can be made into special greeting cards. It should be remembered that working in this way with cloth and thread, the aim is not to produce a naturalistic flower, which can be done in other ways, but merely to suggest the overall freshness and prettiness of the subject.

Diagram 5 Sew the flowers onto the side of the flex frame

GLOSSARY

Bondaweb. Trade name for a glue-backed paper, used for bonding two fabrics together.

Calico. A mid- or heavy-weight natural, pure cotton fabric.

Challis. A pure, fine, woollen fabric.

Fabric glue. This is often a paste glue in stick form, that will readily wash out.

Hessian. A boldly woven jute fabric; not all colours are lightfast.

Lawn. A very fine, soft, pure cotton fabric.

Petersham. A stiff, ribbed, lustrous ribbon, used for stiffening or on its own.

Polycotton. A mixture of polyester and cotton; easy care drip-dry fabric.

Sailcloth. A heavy cotton fabric with a slight rib; can now also be mixed fibres.

Silk habotai. A medium weight pure silk fabric.

Stitch 'N Tear. A felt/paper-like interlining used to back stitchery to prevent it cockling. It can be torn off or allowed to disintegrate.

Tailor tacking. Most machines can be provided with a foot to do this — follow the manufacturer's instructions.

Threads, specialist machine. These can be bought from a sewing machine shop or specialist embroidery supplier (see relevant magazines for addresses). Two manufacturers are: **Madeira**, whose threads include Astro (metallic), Tanne (100% cotton), and rayon in a wide range of single colours and also multicolours. Toledo is a very fine synthetic thread. **Natesh** who make 'Titania' rayon threads in many single and multicolours and 'Empress' which is a gloss thread (i.e. untwisted).

Velcro. A quick form of fastening in 'tape' form. One tape is sewn to one surface and its counterpart to the other. When the two halves are brought together they bond.

Vilene or Pellon. Trade names for a selection of non-fray interlinings of varying weights. The 'iron-on' versions have glue on one side to stick them to the fabric. 'Pelmet' vilene is very stiff, and ideal as a backing for bags or spectacle cases, for example.

INDEX